HOLD HANDS AMONG THE ATOMS

DATE DUE

FEB 2 0 2002	

BRODART   Cat. No. 23-221

Books by Edwin Morgan
published by Mariscat

Grafts/Takes (1983)
Sonnets from Scotland (1984)
Tales from Limerick Zoo (1988)

Edwin Morgan

HOLD HANDS AMONG THE ATOMS

70 poems

Mariscat
1991

ISBN 0 946588 14 7

Acknowledgements are due to the following publications, where some of the poems appeared: *Ambit, Chapman, Cencrastus, Poetry Review, Gown, Spectrum, Gairfish, Gay Scotland, Owl, The Scot-Free Magazine, The Rialto, Orbis, Bête Noire, New Welsh Review, Poetry Ireland Review, New Writing Scotland, Glasgow Herald, Scotsman, Northlight, Outside Lines, Scotland on Sunday, Poetry Book Society Anthology, A Garland for Stephen Spender, Fox.*

The publisher acknowledges subsidy from the Scottish Arts Council towards the publication of this volume.

Cover design by Heather Nevay.
Published by The Mariscat Press, 3 Mariscat Road, Glasgow G41 4ND.
Printed by E.F. Peterson, 12 Laygate, South Shields, Tyne & Wear NE33 5RP.

CONTENTS

There is something to be told about us
for the telling of which we all wait.
                    Laura (Riding) Jackson

            Guman ut scufon,
weras on wilsith wudu bundenne.
            Beowulf

A CHAPTER

They thought they only wanted social justice,
but when it came they caught an unknown sickness.
Oh no there were no marks upon their bodies,
the only pain they said they felt was inward.
Their simple well-cut clothes and well-kept houses,
the well-swept streets and unpolluted highways,
the lifts that worked, the clear blue seas, graffiti
buried under harmonies of paintwork,
were not enough to save them from disfavour,
so they called it, baffled by the absence
of satisfactions they had strained their souls for.
The young ones gathered in tight knots at corners,
an older man would stare across the table
as well-cooked food grew cold, a painful dreaming
sending his spirit through his wife and children
as if they were no more than paper sketches
uselessly interposed before the terrible.
And down among the well-spaced cars and buses
at times a driver would begin to shiver,
put his whole course on automatic, waiting
for something black to fasten on the windscreen
and give him leave to crash in solid blindness.
A generation then began to perish,
wasted by longings in the well-lit cities,
drowned on white beaches where they sat abstracted,
exposed on hilltops under constellations
they strained to glimpse beneath their cloudy burden.
Yet no one knew what laws must have been broken,
or whether their malaise was good or evil.
And that was when they heard the distant shouting.

OCTOBER IN ALBANIA

White kilts and crimson jackets, curvy daggers
and cloaks that might be plaids — a whole Levant of
crypto-Scots — 'I like the Albanians much,' wrote
Byron, had himself painted in their costume.
They still remember him in new Tirana.
Rapid Albanian patter from a guide at
the ethnographic museum became luminous
as he dropped in the magic name and pointed
at dress that might have graced Scotch bards, or pashas.
Belated Sixties flares and decent shirt-sleeves
now, in the bright October heat; no daggers;
they export chrome, hydroelectric power,
tobacco, handmade carpets, rear turkeys,
stroll across carless streets with unwrapped fragrant
loaves, and stare amazed as western strangers
tilt cameras at rooftop neon mantras —
GLORY TO THE PARTY OF LABOUR OF SHQIPËRIA

And what is Shqipëria, land of eagles?
The rebel-roasting pashas have all vanished,
partisan-hanging nazis have all vanished,
all the Zogs and all the gods have vanished.
There's neither star wars here, nor perestroika,
no Hiltons, and no Palaces of Culture,
neither Stolichnaya nor Coca-Cola.
Long narrow mountain-backboned rivery country
of gorge and gully and beach, of pines and roses,
of palms in parks and avenues and gardens
and palms where every gorgeous comb seemed perfect
high on a hill to spread their bearing beauty
over and among the unbearing tombstones
polished in horizontal row on row in
the Cemetery of the Martyrs, soldiers
and partisans of the last hitlerite years, givers
of blood for that most ancient stubborn Illyria.

And one slab, with two armed guards at attention,
a tiny red flag and a twist of flowers,
the very essence of simplicity, said
ENVER HOXHA. Mother Albania breasted
the blue clear air in stone across Tirana.
The white marble plateau was peaceful, silent.
I thought of Scotland's other, shameful silence,
and Mother Scotland like a crone in cast-offs,
breasting nothing; took the steps down, slowly.

A DECADENCE

They knew they'd rather hear two winter tree-tops
clatter and creak than any rut of antlers.
Some even swore by the abandoned whirring
of desultory windmill vanes on headlands,
the miller gone and the cracked millstone grainless.
And those that no one dared to call extremists
said, All we need is dust and a forefinger
and BRANCHES CLASH far better than in forests,
said, All you need is sand, a thumb, and spelt-out
VANES GROAN louder than that wind-blown clockwork.
One day there came a little nutbrown hermit
and found himself a dry and starry cave-mouth.
He told them they no longer needed writing,
no longer needed tree-music, mill-music,
no longer needed venison or bread-rolls,
for everything they did was an evasion
of fact of mind, of (here he smiled) illusion,
and soon there was a yellowing at the edges
as the whole settlement was cracking, curling,
waiting to make a blaze but only smouldering
endlessly, wondering if growing darker
and losing shape and substance would be better
than belling of the brass-voiced fog-rent hungers.

A SALE

The customer is sweating at the counter.
Customers crush behind him, eyes or noses
level with the big man's straining neck-roll.
They elbow to prod into space he's cornered
and snatch at tatty treasures he turns over.
His baggy jumper sleeves flounder and slither
among the baggy jumpers. Paw the tangle
or others will! That fluorescent panting
in the dust-motes! Gloves crawling for clutches!
Wool up to your eyes, the pulling and the hunting,
the dragging of your quarry to the cash-desk,
the bulging carrier-bag, the bags, the three bags,
and oh the credit, the escalators, the exits
into streets like slowly moving walkways
packed customer-tight, a marathon of inches
towards the bus lanes and the darkening suburbs:
it is the custom, customers; the custom.

AN ISLAND

Heavy as rum and sweeter than molasses
that island pitched its clam-shells into waters
blue and gently shelving, swum-in, sharkless.
The sticklike centenarian storytellers —
there were some three of them at easy reckoning —
invaded barbecues and lulled the feasters
(as wild pig and clam devils drowned in kava
glistened through the pores of bored teenagers)
with histories of their forefathers' heroes
drawing up war canoes on sands they reddened
with axed princes and gorging their parched throats
with wild pig and clam devils drowned in kava.
To hell with war, the young men thought, as gobbets
of gristle tickled their plump chests, and pissing
through their loin-cloths made a raucous pastime.
Unsteady girls were shrieking between hiccups.
The storytellers tottered into hammocks.
Unadmired, the never less than brilliant
stars began to prick the dark. And never
a squeak from stuck princes. A Pacific Homer
was itching strongly to be born, oh he'd be
bringing in the dead drunk, burned on fire-stones,
and high-tide-drowned slumped boys like gods, and vomit
slurped from coconuts by fuddled fathers
who retched with terror as a raw-boned morning
hit them from somewhere in the universe they
thought it was a mercy to have forgotten.

A CEREMONY

Stout bollards and red cones provide corrals for
visitors of curiosity and distinction.
The bunting flies in bright but tasteful pastels.
Cool awnings wait for any faint observers.
The ritual of Trampling on the People
is annual, public, ancient, and instructive,
and draws large throngs into the Square of Squares for
reasons imaginable and unimaginable.
All traffic is forbidden, and a thousand
citizens from the peripheral favelas
lie prostrate and quite naked on the asphalt
with stiff arms by their sides. The heat beats fiercely.
A hundred of the great ones of the region,
some dripping with imperial insignia,
some plainly suited in grey polyester,
some few with masks, though that was hardly needful,
and all smart-booted, cuban-heeled, spurred, studded,
descend from their ungaudy valanced platform.
A midday cannon galvanized the phalanx
to strut along the backs the high sun offered,
crisscrossing in the carefullest formation
till none escaped the heel and the dispassion
which ground knees, bellies, nipples, lips, and foreheads
briefly into the stony earth they came from.
At a command, the tramplers regained their dais.
A further cannon-shot, and the bruised beings
stumbled erect in silence, and dispersing
into the streets and avenues with neither
clothes nor shame at lack of them, gave nature
more than human power had dispossessed there,
while jaunty music froze our very spirit
into vows that set like iron, and bound us.

A STATUE

The statue was manhandled down quite slowly
for safety's sake, being so huge and heavy,
and hundreds more than had been reckoned likely
came to stare and shout and spit and cheer those
businesslike demolishers. Then they were dancing
on fallen concrete epaulettes, a shoulder,
a block of rain-black cheek where the split face had
burst and spilt no blood or brain, no anything
apart from rusty rods that mocked each human
backbone with their undestroyed reminder
of iron laws and iron men; dance! tear them!
By nightfall, all had gone. The broken pieces
lay huddled under an uneasy moonlight.
Clouds trailed their gravecloths. Shots cracked, though faintly.
One by one, muffled scuttling figures gathered
among the ruins and began to pocket fragments,
melting off quickly into the dark. None gestured,
none spoke. A knuckle, an ear-lobe, a button
vanished to unknown cupboards and shoe-boxes,
not ikons for diehards but mere mementoes
of bad times those who took them hardly dreamed of
returning, except that they did dream it, later,
making their children finger a few ugly
shards of pain that never can be buried.

PERSUASION

You never thought much of the darkness, did you?
You wanted everything so open, open —
I said it could not be — you laughed, and shook me,
and pointed me and swivelled me to windows,
doors, rivers, skies — said it must be, must issue
right out if it was to have any honour —
what: love? — yes: love; it must seal up its burrow,
must take a stair or two, a flight or two, for
poles, horizons, convoys, elevations —
but tender still to backcourts and dim woodlands.
Oh, never ask where darkness is if light can
break down the very splinters of the jambs — be
sure I know you can take in the sunlight
through every pore and nothing will be blinded
or shrivelled up like moth in flame or crippled
by some excess of nakedness — just give it,
your intelligence, your faith I really mean, your
faith, that's it, to see the streets so brilliant
after gales you really can go out there,
you really can have something of that gladness,
many things under the sun, and not disheartened,
so many in their ways going beside you.

AN OFFER

Imagine all the sea was turned to money,
lapping the shore with notes and twinkling silver,
how many do you think would jump the pierhead,
or hire a hovercraft to waft it closer,
or drown, scrabbling with sacks through miles of paper?
The maddened gulls and guillemots are starving,
the stalled propellers vainly scrunching millions,
the submarines clank under squalls of quarters,
the blinded bathysphere has ten-pound windows.
Imagine when this wealth has turned to coral,
and banks of it rise up, as sharp as razors,
and children with unwary feet are bleeding
as they scamper on the ghosts of long-dead deutschmarks.
What would you pay to have a new convulsion
send the reefs roaring to greed-grey Avernus?

AN ELEGY

Nil-nisi-bonum-bloody-Hirohito,
amiable plankton dissector, never doubted
prisoners should have well-defined rib-cages,
contours not shrouded by superfluous flesh-rolls,
you had to see the slavery, it was stoic,
sunken eyes and stick legs, not statistics,
you had to hear the beaten scream, and sometimes
that faintest plump of entrails on the concrete,
large white barbarians, and so they were too
as happened, were the odds evened in ovens
of nuclear fire? Electronic gardens
and a cherry-tree and no weapons, fine now
is it? Whales to be culled only for science?
All's-well-that-ends-well-Akihito, bowing
to his father's chrysanthemums, has need of nightmares
we can only give him in poems, even
from the other side of the world, and even
from another world than this if there was one, where
shades, if there were shades, would gather singing
matters the living cannot quite yet sing of,
lacking the desolation of those dead ones.
But what we can we write, here, Hirohito.

HANDS ON, 1937

John S. Clarke, festooned with snakes, said, 'Touch one,
look closely, they're quite beautiful; not slimy;
come on, come down to the front now, that's better.
Don't be afraid, girls, aren't these eyes pure jewels?
Come on lads, stretch your hands out, try this johnny,
I bet it's like no creature you ever handled.'
I thought the lecture had been good, but this was
unforeseen, an unknown world, strange bonus —
the dry brown coil was at first almost leaden,
slightly rough but inert, with scales tight-fitting
like Inca walls, till what seemed a faint tickling
became a very crawling of the flesh as
movement began to test my arm, the ripples
of an almost unfathomable power
rhythmically saying, I am living:
you may not love me but oh how I am living!
And it is all one life, in tanks, bags, boxes,
lecture-theatres, outhouses, fronds of bracken,
rivers for men and serpents to swim over
from dark bank to dark bank and vanish quickly
about their business in raw grass and reedland,
scale, sole, palm, tail, brow, roving, brushing, touching.

A DRAGON

We brushed out suddenly and very roughly
from the black thicket, sweating, angry, filthy,
adventurers dishevelled to our toecaps —
oh yes we had our boots, for snakes and leeches —
still trailing all that sodden gear, tents, ponchos,
machetes almost blunt with hacking, bugles
bashed and drowned and merely ornamental —
when we saw what was not an open country —
oh that would be too simple for our masters
up there, if there are any, we don't think so —
but only an incomparable garden
we gingered into with an uncouth shyness,
tugging shirts into belts, pretending order,
whistling then desisting, cut turf a wonder,
lakes, little Turkish kiosks, laurel bowers,
vetiver-scented fountains — who would dare to
break such glassy arches with the grime we'd
gathered in our trudging mangrove trances?
We stuttered down to love-seats; air was gentle;
abstraction took us one by one as listening
to a bird — unknown — sing three clear notes descending
in inhuman not sad not happy sweetness,
we sat a while like unfinished statues, knowing
our caravanserai was not for gardens.

Only later we learned there was a dragon,
often not present, always sometimes present,
not to be calculated. Papery arbours
whisper softly. Gardeners with light wheelbarrows
trundle themselves home to wife and children,
not even glancing at what must be evening
drawing dark wings high over the poplars.

But fountain jets are steam by midnight. Chaos
blows stacked bricks through the screaming cottage cradles.
Something very old is at large, breathing.
A single violet is an irritation
so intense that it is burnt to ashes,
the ashes stamped to dust, and the dust roared at
till not a particle could find its neighbour.
They say it is in pain, to cause such havoc.
We doubt it — but we are only fighters.
We should have stayed there, should have stood there, comrades!

THE LAST INTIFADA

It seems a sunny window morning murmur
with arms on sills. You sense the trembling house-plants
as planes roar past below the radar, bringing
safety and terror. Non-existent trumpets
are heard to take the lid off some repair-shop.
You speak, everyone speaks, the dusty city
is like a bush of sparrows. The streets are filling,
and now what might be nearhand seas — it's not though —
are breaking, crashing, seething back, and breaking.
Where is the throne? Where are the iron gods then,
with their gold racks and fiery chairs, tormentors
and cowardly commanders, is it bunkers,
morions, pretorians, doors dead to keypads?
Blisters travel on their grounded gunships.
What are the iron gates once they are broken?
Whose is the throne that makes a little firewood?
What happened to the gods that found a million —
oh no, not money, but a million people —
swarming over their guards and gravely singing,
sternly singing but with grave exultation,
stern assurance, a strange forward movement
that cut a swathe like a sea surge, the voices
rising and falling and the high sun shining?
They're dying. They are dying, they are dying.

AN ABANDONED CULVERT

The daffodils sang shrill within the culvert.
Their almost acid notes amazed the darkness
culverts are happiest with. They could not cower,
the yellow birds, pure cries on stilts, conundrums
to burst the reason of those mineral courses.
Five stubborn half-fluted half-ragged non-fluting trumpets
blared the dank brickfall grit into submission.
Whatever daffodils can say, they said it
louder and sharper than the stalagmites they
might have been, if all the timorous ages
had managed to conspire against some thrusting
of the dumb seed that could not know, yet knew, it
had to unapologetically
proclaim a yellow and not golden treasure
unyielding to the kisses of the digger.

A CITY

— What was all that then? — What? — *That.* — That was *Glasgow.*
It's a film, an epic, lasts for, anyway
keep watching, it's not real, so everything is
melting at the edges and could go, you have to
remember some of it was shot in Moscow,
parts in Chicago, and then of course the people
break up occasionally, they're only graphics,
look there's two businessmen gone zigzag, they'll be
off-screen in one moment, yes, I thought so.
— What a sky though. — Ah well, the sky is listed,
change as it may. It's a peculiar platinum
with roary sunset flecks and fissures, rigging
was best against it, gone now, don't regret it,
move on, and if you wait you'll see some children,
oh it's a fine effect, maybe they're real, some
giant children pulling down a curtain
of platinum and scarlet stuff as airy
as it seems strong, and they'll begin to play there,
bouncing their shrill cries till it's too dark to
catch a shadow running along the backcloth,
and they still won't go home, despite the credits.
— You mean the film goes on, beyond the credits?
— You'll have to wait and see, won't you? It's worth it.
— I'm not persuaded even of its existence.
— What, *Glasgow?* — The city, not the film. — The city
is the film. — Oh come on. — I tell you. — Right then,
look. Renfield Street, marchers, banners, slogans.
Read the message, hear the chant. — Lights! Camera!
— But where are the children? — That I grant you;
somewhere, huge presences; shouting, laughter;
hunch-cuddy-hunch against a phantom housewall.

A SMOKEHOUSE

The smokehouse girl was talking to the salmon.
Go down, come up, get on that rack, my beauty.
You'll not be leaping on this smoky ladder.
Just listen to the wood-chips quietly fuming,
and oh if you could tap that barrel you'd be
swimming in the smell of sweeter forests
than any you nudged warily through reed-beds.
Money in purse is sweeter still. No poacher
will slip your rosy goldy squeeze-packed meltings
in his mouth. Receptions with a touch of lemon
will strike up, and a glass of something, burst of
well-bred strings. Swim in that, you stupid
creature! Flies have hooks when they're too perfect,
your mother must have told you. What, she didn't?
Can't you watch shadows? I think you're as greedy
as we are, even when you see the line you
snatch the lure, as if a gulp could render
the impending less terrible or fortify the present
with food that chokes on air. Keep smoking will you!
Turn that squashed eye away. I need my wages.
Who is on the rack at Achiltibuie?

IL TRAVIATO

That's my eyes at their brightest and biggest.
It's belladonna. I've a friend who. Not that
I'd ever use too much, did once, came out of
delirium after a week of sweats, you learn. But
I'm so pale now, some men like the contrast
as I stand in the park with my eyes burning,
or glide among the poplars, they're thin as I am
but seem to manage, get their light, get nourished
as I get trade although the Wraith's my nickname.
I ought to be in bed, probably, maybe.
In any case my lover sends me out now,
he says it's all I'm good for, bring some money.
He hides my razor till I'm 'interesting',
a chalky portrait ruffed in my black stubble.
I mustn't be too hard on him. The years we.
It all comes down to what kind of constant
you believe in, doesn't it, not mathematics
but as if you had the faintest brilliance
that was only yours, not to let any sickness
douse it, or despair creeping with a snuffer.
I sometimes think I wish it could be ended
— those hard-faced brutes that hit you at the climax —
but then I go on, don't I, as everyone
should, pressing through the streets with glances
for all and everything, not to miss crumbs of
life, drops of the crowded flowing wonder.

DIFFERENCE

The endless variousness is all for praises.
The faces, passing, never make an empire.
And Iskander stopped writing in Abkhazian,
Aigi in Chuvash, Rytkheu in Chukcha.
So much the worse, so much the worse. You think not?
You'd rather have the second-best as long as
millions get it? — Mission, you cry, the mission!
we want the mass to move en bloc, not crunch on
caltrops, inessentials, unideals!
We catch an awkward squad we do a brainwash
with promises of universal favour
far beyond the sheep-fanks, fish-holes, shamans.
Why not — it's easy — cut fish-holes in Russian?
— The endless variousness evolves, the empire
expires in frozen edicts, you can skate there
but soon you're off the edge, and then there's no one
bar the unassimilated — *bar-bar, bar-bar* —
to save you, and why should they, since you doomed them
to hold their tongue, and everything that made them
to their hearts, flags burning a locked drawer,
songs that are not alien to the alien,
accreted stinging stories mocking labials
where you are a *bar-bar* to them. The faces
pass, the individuals, how there can be such
difference we do not know but what we do know
is that an absolute instinct loves it different,
the world, the dialectic, the packed coaches
whistling at daybreak through the patched countries.

A PASTORAL

The glen, the dene, the chine, the dell, the leasowe —
a world of secrets goes about its business
and never needs to tell you until maybe
when you lie drowsing in the summer murmur
a cow snorts and a quick hoof-splinter flashes
colours and lights in the low water-meadow
and you say Oh I can't doze, I must remember.
The hoofs move and the rings break and the colours
dapple those soggy shallows so demandingly,
the big head droops and puffs and slops, shakes drops off,
trundles its bulk after it, brindling damply,
dunly happy, chewing so half-abstractedly,
you might think messages that very midday
were coming at you, but you can't remember
even though you sat up with your eyes shaded,
ants running off in panic, the smell of grasses
deliriously clovery, the sweets and greens and breathings
round you and in you, an almost silent Woodstock
where, yes that's it, throw off, you can be naked
as an ant, pick your way among not lovers
with their beads and smoke, but even closer secrets,
weeds disregarded, rainbows you must wade through.
Everything would give everything to be remembered.

DAYS

Where have those long days gone that used to charm us
before we knew we could be discontented?
I said the grass was waves, my toy boat bobbing.
To get the swishing sound I thought was sea was
steady tugs on the string. We made a mortal
soup then in a bent bowl, dandelions, burnwater,
curls of dropped catkins, what not else, mullocked it
about, had just the sense to sip not swallow.
Was it sun or clouds, who knows, that was for grown-ups.
We'd hours with roadmenders, their hut forbidden
and so a place of great resort, a dusty
sweaty sweary tarry magic caravan,
they quizzed us, shared their cans of tea, felt our
no muscles and laughed, surrounded us like a story
of familiar giants we'd never be afraid of.
The time that must have come and gone was faces
at windows, angry shouts from doorways, this minute,
come in, until we too could sense the shadows
advancing with what must be the end. Scliffing
the pavement, throwing burrs, they have to, slowly,
the children, come home, where all the clocks are racing.

A NEEDLE

They'll find it in the haystack, the good needle.
The straw house may be stars rings strings eclipses
and nothing going straight can pierce the jungle
of dimensions and no expedition not carrying
time with them in a bag can hope to live through
tight-forked tick-filled random-steaming centuries
and navigators and their sons and daughters
may feel fate rather than some constellation
is stacked against them and a radioactive
hand may scrabble palsied at the panel
when ships are briefly bucked by something grimmer
than light and even though some one or two should
lock into hopeless madness and be ejected
and black religions come and go in phases
to induce despair and dazzling mathematicians
clutch at straws and smoke them and so sleepwalk:
when all is said and done it can't be hidden,
it glints among a nebula in ruins,
it holds itself among the suns, its patience
sits among the dust-clouds that can tarnish
everything less than goodness; invisible
it cannot be but long unseen and longing
to be seen: oh yes and to be used, to swoop through
wounds it would knit, banners to be invested
with futures of things known, frames to be figured
to hopes as iron as Homer's woman fed on,
against the odds of being only human.

A VANGUARD

We came to the end of the world at midnight.
Someone called out from the back of the column,
Is that it then? What is it like? I answered,
Whatever you have of imagination
you must use. Come forward. All of you. Stand easy.
Through so much dust, we were no smart company,
but somehow the tired group seemed monumental
as any old stone circle where they clustered
gravely over staves and rifles and brooded
above the yelling abyss we'd reached the lip of.
And those who thought a globe could never have one —
abyss, I mean, edge, rim, sick slope to vacancy —
began to shiver at celestial mechanics
crumbling away. It must be a ravine then,
fog, darkness, the farther bank is hidden —
one of them said, using imagination.
No one believed that rational man; the spirit
of the place, our chilling sweat, the terrible groaning
from throats unseen below our feet, took toll of
any reason we had left. What had we looked for
in fact but the end of the world, we the vanguard
sent out to scotch or seal appalling rumours.
So there we were. Was it hell? We saw no one.
The cold grew more intense. Let's go back then,
I said, it's not the end of the world. Joking
broke the spell. Someone laughed. A ravine surely,
windy caves and flues like voices. And supper
a short march away. Soon they would start whistling.
I kept my thoughts, but nothing would do, nothing.
No end in time was near, or in space possible.
As for the dead, who am I to appease them,
a scout, a ragged man, a storyteller?

AUNT MYRA (1901–1989)

A horse in a field in a picture is easy.
A man in a room with a fan, we wonder.
It might be whirring blades in steamy downtown —
but no, it's what she's left beside her dance-cards.
How she sat out a foxtrot at the Plaza
and fanned her brow, those far-off flirty Twenties
he opens and shuts with an unpractised gesture
that leaves the years half-laughing at the pathos
of the clumsy, until rising strings have swept them
dancing again into silence. The room darkens
with a blue lingering glow above the roof-tops
but the man still stands there, holding up the dangling
dance-cards by their tiny attached pencils.
The cords which are so light seem to him heavy
as if they were about to take the strain of
tender evenings descending into memory.
Something is hard, not easy, though it's clearly
a man, a fan, a woman, a room, a picture.

A CABAL

The hard men of the orchestra are certain.
Even two tears for music's two too many.
What you must wrap yourself around is texture.
Dry yourself out like jeans on spikes of structure.
And you must call a violin a fiddle,
les sanglots longs des violons kept under.
They can all spot a whining *rallentando*
from afar, take it as briskly as they dare to.
They like a pounding chug (more where that came from).
If directionality's not in your dictionary
it should be. The well-made, unmanned goalposts
loom ready to shoot into with a wallop.
Conductor-referees can flap and harrow,
unshaken audiences demand refunds for
absence of injury-time. The hard men calmly
sew it up, troop out, coats on, taxi. Where to,
squire? *An die Musik, bitte.* But he never made it.

MORNING IN NAPLES

At six in the morning, in the empty side-street
I waited for the motor to the airport:
cool pigeon-whirring Sunday, early stillness
of the manic city, a white cat on the cobbles
going home, an ancient jangle from a tower
just seen, cracked wall behind cracked wall, a flourish
of indomitable weeds in the high stonework
and then the freshness, the faintly stirring silence
of the lightening blue overhead uncloudedly
arching out east to veiled Vesuvius.
The bag at my feet was perfect: all transience,
all pause, all flight, all as out of time as
the bells were out of tune, and as I stood there
watching for a white car I was not watching
for anything but a world beginning over,
over and over without a blurt of trumpets,
up from the bay sea haze with the Greek founders
until unlikely now, uneven pavement,
paw and claw on stone and peal in sunshine,
and me unsweating yet, but still uncertain
as one car seems to slow, and yes, she's waving.
I lift my bag, she stops, the spell is broken.
We sped through the no traffic. Conversation
streamed out behind us like a scarf, or banner,
or something else we were busily transferring
into an insatiable distance.

FRIDAY

Hammer and Sickle, a Communist party weekly,
is to be renamed *Friday*.
                              (news item, September 1989)

Goodbye to industry, good riddance to agronomy,
wave them off with two fingers, mothball
the combine harvesters and the cream separators,
parcel your scuffed overalls and loamy wellingtons
to the third world, switch off, lock up, go fallow,
wipe your graphs and targets from the blackboard,
production's dirty, petrol stinks, bread chokes you,
live on air and water and *Imagine*,
don't go to heaven, don't believe in anything,
melt down your videos and glut the Baltic
with blown-up library rubble, watch dogs hunting
through Lenin's tomb for a last yellow gigot
and get your lasers trained upon the diorite,
give the pomp a touch of nigromancy,
whistle the pulverized granite over Tallin,
see people swallow one another up like
dolls and roll the monster to a coal-pit
where chains hang dead and nothing shrugs the dust off:
but still you can't do anything with Friday,
can't eat it, read it, drink it, cut grass with it,
it won't knock nails or rivets in, won't make your
next ice-cream, or lover's ring, or ticket
for that new film about a revolution,
it can live only in its bland abstraction
from all the hard things that are great in hardness,
the setbacks that still sting us crying forwards,
it has no face, and only an illusion
of a smile, it beckons, but you must not buy it.

A MEMORIAL

Stupendous days of unattended toilets!
bright eye-devouring afternoons, hesit-
ancies of dusk, rustle and whisper of midnights
where sometimes the full moon would make a sculpture
of two close heads as it worked through a grating,
or absolute eye-prickling foggy blackness
would let divine touch heal the lonely, leaven
the ugly, foreground the age-old desperations;
and locals would stroll round on sunny mornings
with dog or crossword, oh, half-honestly but
not without a flickering eye. By Kelvin waters,
by Liffey waters we watched the shadows gather,
heard those hoarse commands that were entreaties,
caught a match sputtering, cupped hands, a cheekbone,
waited timeless as the sullen flotsam
wandered below to all-receiving ocean.

Sometimes a padlocked door remains, more often
a demolished space, or emptiness refilled with
seats, a shelter, a kiosk, some trees; even
a real cottage: and the wind whistles round it.
No plaques will be forthcoming, only poems,
only the voices you hear in poems. Where are
the groans and sighs and bowls of cream? They're playing
other halls, when they can find them. It's harder
when liberal laws ensure the lawless places
are outlawed: so much for progress. Memory
hoists its flesh, its shambles, like a standard.

AN INTERVIEW

'What did you see when they unrolled the bandage?'
'Everything was very grey and crumbly.
I did lift an arm, it was like a dead thing,
dropped right back; I thought that was terrible.
And the stench, to know it was your own, Jesus!'
'Speaking of whom, did he come back to see you?'
'Not he. He's like all shamans, do the job and
get the glory. He's off preaching somewhere.
Here am I with eyes like pits, limbs twitching,
clothes falling off me, sisters wailing, children
running from me in the street I'm so gruesome —
children I love, running away, you call this
living? What does he know about living?'
'Do you agree with those who wish to kill him?'
'Surely that is what he wants? We know them
these holy men, death-bringers even when they're
bringing the dead to life. They crucify the spirit.
He has destroyed a family for his greatness.'
'Some would say you really should be thankful.'
'Thankful for what? Look at me: a stick-insect.
Martha burnt the shroud. I scrubbed myself but
without purchase. I still smell those spices
that make the fetor worse. We are all dying
but is this to be borne, this death, this solitude?'
'Finally, have you a message for our readers?'
'Roll the stone right over me the next time.'

A DEPARTURE

Before we left, we sat down like old Russians,
breathed steadily till none of us was anxious
any more, and our packed gear seemed gold-foiled
in the low sun, like gifts. We held our helmets
loose in our laps. The place had a great quietness,
the marble floor, the porch, the little fountain.
Nothing escapes from time, but it was like that.
We looked out where the universe was slanting
off and down, bright, full of forms, quite distant
but then very near and to be reached. Our captain
nodded, rose, we rose, put on our helmets.
It was vincible now, that illimitable.

URBAN GUNFIRE

'Civilians' are not really, truly, people.
As regimes fall, they're only 'caught in crossfire'.
Expendablest of the expendable, they
crawl, or if they're lucky someone drags them,
to doorways where they slump and shake till nightfall.
How great it must be not to be civilian
or anything but gun in hand, young, mobile,
slogan-fuelled better than machines are,
you cannot even hear the shattered housewife,
far less see her blood and bags and bread, it's
bullet time between you and your sniper,
hot streaks go shopping, nothing else goes shopping,
no one is out there in the open, we are,
we are it and it is where they vanish
like a clapped piece of tawdry human magic,
too feeble to be seen by psyched-up fighters.
Their cries are in another world. The trigger
is steady as they roll about the tarmac.
And it goes on as if it could not finish.

A WARNING

What makes you think you have an acclamation?
Was it, they dragged the body of socialism
into a common grave, quicklime, dancing,
opening of cathedrals, minuet of
vestments as they cross the ancient incense,
ranks of dew-eyes dibbling trembling candles
in waxbound trays that never will grow freedom?
Musty but indefatigable reaction
stirs half-incredulously on one elbow
in another tomb as the bells clang, whistles,
laughs, clacks his grubby bones and orders suitings,
modest, subfusc, meeting the *novus ordo*
with decency. What, a republic a kingdom?
No no, there's nothing waiting in the wings, it's
early days. Take your string bag. An orange
will appear by magic, steaks, heroin, tickets
for strippers. Don't feel bought, you're buying, buying.
— And if, oh, if any should stint the euphoria
for a moment, watching the snow falling slowly
over shot-pocked facades, there'd only be some
muffled echo of the better life that
never seems to come, like a faint singing
heard in the pauses of snoring out of cardboard
or waiters' shouts from bursting blood-red kitchens.
They must listen so very hard, the freed ones!

A NIGHT SWEAT

I slept at last. It was a night of panthers.
In and out of something labyrinthine
which might have been bamboos, the smoky slinkers
appeared and disappeared, kept all their terror
tight, never looked to left or right, circled
finally (I knew they must) the tree I crouched in.
One head (that was enough) rocked, sniffed, swung upward,
flashed me a glare to melt tree-trunks, was part of
a mechanism that sketched more crawl than
spring up the bole and as if tentatively
clawed my overhanging leg and raked it
to tatters. What a shout it was I snatched it
back with, woke with, sweating, both hands clutching
the king of cramps, the furrowed spasm stretching
my very toes like claws, the panther's sinews
within me like a transplant, the pulsing ripples
of slowly untwisting muscles suddenly jerking
again and again, six, seven times, into searing
tautness as I tried to squirm the pain off
under the sheet or over the blanket (im-
possible, I know, you wait, you stick it).
There was a kind of morning in the offing,
an hour or so away. I was hardly breathing
as the last twitch subsided, had to dare to
move, exhausted into sweet relief that
turned me on the other side from panthers
(I hoped, and so it was). I slept to traffic
rolling by on its most ordinary business.

A STORY

Once upon a time there was a story.
(Listen, children. Listen, wind. Listen, curtains.)
The story went to sea and stowed its oilskins.
It caught a fish farm and a cat-o-nine-tails,
a dog watch and some Mother Carey's chickens,
a donkey jacket and a weevil biscuit.
One night as it was swinging in its hammock,
tapping its darling tin of Golden Virginia
with one hand, while the other hand was trailing
down into the throbbing darknesses that
gathered to lick it, something quite gigantic
clamped itself to the keel and churned the vessel
round and down and round and down to drown there,
with hammocks catching fish, and fish tobacco.
The story had inflated its bright oilskins
and with a leap of most uncommon power
soared up and out over the waves, discharging
weak wet zigzag flashes in the moonlight.
Dawn found it shrinking, battered, leaky, falling,
dipping at last into the sea. The story
was now so small it hopped into a bottle
bobbing on a patch of phosphorescence.
On the Broomielaw I picked it up, and brought it
home (O curtains, O wind) and read its message
once upon a time (O children). How happy
it was it told me that homecoming ending.

TWILIGHTS

The darker darkness we have means to deal with,
it is the lighter darkness that confounds us,
the twilight of not knowing, the grey weighing,
the waiting, undisclosed and undisclosing,
the no day and the no night and the sickening
pause, the slow precipitate of phantoms.
Fog that fills the boat is worse than water.
I've seen some baling it hysterically
as if they could force out the imponderable —
they can't. Oh you must make a show of patience
even when patience is so hard to muster.
Soon you can see reluctant demons fading;
it must be something they can't stand; they're twisting
in their malevolent pain but they're transparent,
they're being entered, filled by something lighter,
they're being killed by what can only now be
sunlight, yes it's daybreak, the horizon
is like a seed-pod bursting to deliver
its one red melting fiery convex fruit-head,
loading the waves with those re-offered promises
of paths to take to brightness and best landfalls.
And such a loud wind fills the sails we're blustered
out of ourselves into a world of daylight,
of ropes, and spray, and clouds running and running.

A SKEW

They proved the theory of surplus matter
by finding almost infinitely tiny
traces of the pipe the universe was
blown from, like a vase in Venice. Fragments
ranging through a dozen constellations
gave out at last a strangely twisted oval,
as if the blower had once been a jailbird,
blew as he spoke, with half his mouth. Onward,
the astronomers cried, fine, who needs a circle?
Better to live like flies in a bashed rummer
sweetened with fresh beer-dregs and froth-splotches
than skate a smiling perfect disc — incisive —
twice — three times — and drown. So they made merry
in orbit and on the mountain-tops, preparing
news of the skews, that was the phrase, for broadcast,
leaving the darker question of what prison
the gaunt primordial glassblower had starved in
before escaping to produce such matter
as he'd have wished a hundred times robuster
though not more perfect, if in imperfection
starriest anti-handedness prevailed there.

A DEFENCE

I am told I should not love him, the magpie,
that he's a bully, but then I watch them bouncing
along the grass, chattering, black and white and
he and she, twigs in beak, the tree-top swaying
with half a nest in a hail-shower, the magpies
seeing off crows and gulls — a feint of mobbing
but who knows — eyeing a lost swan waddling
down the pavement, off course from Bingham's waters,
the smart bright bold bad pairing caring magpies
whose nest was blown down last December, back now
to build again, to breed again, to bring us
a batch of tumbling clockwork liquorice allsorts,
spruce, spliced, diced, learning to prance and hurtle
through evening and morning sycamores with what must be
something like happiness, the magpies, cocky,
hungry, handsome, an eye-catching flash for that
black and white collie to bark at, and the black and
white cat lurking under the car-bonnet
to lash a bushy tail at, and this page, seeing
these things, first white, now white and black, to pay its
tribute to, and lay out, thus, its pleasure.

THE LAST PIRAGUA

Well gouged and shaved, well balanced and well painted,
the last piragua left the drum-beats dying
as it slid out over our dark still river.
Standing rowers poling through the lilies —
black statues only just come to life — measured
their movements with such nonchalance of knowledge
that a gear-change would have seemed crude and tasteless —
oh such late voyagers can afford perfection!
For both the rowers and the rowed were standing,
talking at ease, gauging the slightest gesture,
the closest thing to walking on the water
a low-slung log could have devised for watchers.
The moon struggled through mangroves. They sang it
the last ballad, which was not sad, but steady
like everything they did, as if tomorrow
would see them pulled up at some village landfall
with dogs and children, melons rolled in ginger.
But nothing now was to be ordinary.
Soon they must reach the delta, choose the channel,
smell the ocean. Soon I must stretch slowly,
turn in, hang up my binoculars, listen
to I hardly know what life quietly rustling
through overgrown veranda straw, unsleeping
as I shall be unsleeping, drifting to waters
where I hardly know what grandeurs glisten,
or where my hut on stilts would walk me over,
or under, crying out, I saw the rowers!
I cannot die if I have seen the rowers!

A SUNSET

Long rays take our long gaze out westward,
seaward, to the end of the city in waters,
almost dissolving thought in a drown of colours
where all definition would struggle to surface
from its puny swim of orange and crimson,
till something wrests us back, arrests the dreaming,
wrenches and clenches the body to face eastward:
the hospital's nine storeys are so fiery
it is a jolt to credit a reflection
with power to make one blank glass wall a blazing
cage for prisoner-patients to shout out from,
or so we'd think, with knotted sheets, their bedsteads
melting behind them, a jagged cry coming over —
but everything is calm, the brilliance fading
minute by minute into that absence
which is the ward only of imagination
uncurtains other pains and other panics
in real Gartnavel General, but leaving
a little warmth and sun, a little healing.

A FEAST

— But what am I to do with all these pumpkins?
— Bowl them to Hollywood to feed the turkeys!
— You know they fell from off the back of a — ?
— No defence is needed. Sock it to them!
— Zombie pie and mumbling stew of cowboys?
— Have a slice of choking psychomania!
— Chew the creepy seeds of bloodless mutants?
— Bake a child of outer space for supper!
— A brunch of sleaze, well buttered in its batter?
— And one enormous car-chase tart for afters!
— But have we got the stomach for such crumbles?
— They've colourized the black and white, it's magic!
— Can you just wait to wolf that yellow ribbon?
— All those dark brown low-slung twitchy holsters!
— That brush-off in the heaving flesh-tint swimsuit?
— And one last slurp of siren-haunted sidewalk!
— Pyramids of punkins! Shall we bang them westward?
— Cram the turkeys. It's business and it's movies!

AN ARGUMENT

'Whoever heard of a line ending *poem?*'
'You'd rather have the thud of *door-knob, jam-jar?*'
'Disgusting self-reflexiveness, I'd send it
packing.' 'I ask again, you want a *pick-axe?*'
'I want the line to get out and to stay out.'
'Walking through the universe one morning
I came across a cryptically clinging,
then tingling, singing tumbleweed, blown down there
as many ages as the wind had, fashioned
by sand as if it had been half hand-fashioned
and who knows if it was, the intricacies
were balled to figures like a sweated carving,
landscapes no less if you had eyes to mark them.
I held it light as a wish, would not have crushed it
for all the chisels, hammers, time-clocks, profits
it was not made from. I brought it through the desert —
you follow? — placed it here, not on this table
you're drumming at — why are you so impatient? —
but here, in line, where it becomes a poem.'
'What happened to the tumbleweed for chrissake?'
'I let it go of course; lovely; still tumbling.'

A VISIT

There's another. That's another. And another.
They seem to come to us from their own country
as if they loved us, or found something sustaining
in roofs and woods, airs of blue and pavements,
waters still and wild. Whether they have nothing,
or have become tired of whatever brilliance
it was they swooped from, or are merely knocking
by chance on this world's half-hinged storm-door
because they saw a gleam inside that teased them,
or heard some engine-puttering that pleased them,
there's nothing in our universe to tell us.
If you want help, you must undo your secrets!
If you attack us, we shall not be gentle!
And yet you seem to come and go uncaring,
strangers to solicitation, travelling
who knows what endless circuits that must break here
as briefly to you as we might watch a paper
we cannot read caught on some swirling freeway
before it gusts off white through wastelands into
air and vanishes among the cloud-banks.

A QUESTION

They were so anxious, yet they had some spirit.
Some of them shook their fists at us, though mostly
they plodded, scurried, frowned about their business
as we'd been told they would. What was most striking
was that things did hold, the many intersections
did somehow flow through one another, order
without calm did seem to work, not always —
we saw their blood, and bits — but surely something
had ground together in a great coherence —
they could not see it, but we did, we could see it —
over a few hundred thousand years of using
their planet, well, badly, up, no matter,
we know and they know there are others waiting
for spade and drill and geodesic dome. Well then,
but why is it not that, but this, this only
I cannot relegate, forget, make sense of,
how one of them stood there intently watching —
he was not young, not a fool — a piece of newspaper
caught in traffic, blown then across wastelands,
up among clouds where — and that's all — it vanished?

A SLING

A figure came slowly out of the forest
with a child. She was in rags and had been crying
but that was over. Her glance was like steel to
those watching. The boy in his blue coat gathered
her wrist where it had been hanging loosely, not for
protection or out of fear but as if her body
was not his mother but a graven weapon
he would sling willing hard inexplicable
against the perpetrators, the oppressors.
He would say nothing, but he would see them crying.
Their cursed horses curvet, clash their stirrups.

A PARTICULAR COUNTRY

No philosophers darkened that country.
Decreation, deconstruction died there
in the hot loamy burst of seedlings, squabs' teeth
cracking shells in zigzags, rain-forests
torn to shreds by squawks and shrieks that left them
untorn. As for general ideas,
a blowpipe picked them off, they joined the leaf-mould
to mulch minute minuter and minutest
particulars. Watered silk had nothing
on those vibrancies, creakings, thrustings, scatterings,
splash and flicker, drop and web, smudge and whirr, endless
intermitted unpredictable form-crinklings,
rhubarb-clumps with peacocks in a downpour,
what a sparkle of lushnesses, what a catmint
to roll in, what a maze of eyes to thread, that
mass of change and chance and challenge where you
go out; sink in; draw deep at signs that daze you
as stock might, in the nights of your own country.

A COACH-TOUR (J.G.S.)

You did not know it, but nothing you could do to me
was worse than your silence when you were angry.
Often when I did wrong as a boy, my parents
refused the release of storming it out, pretended
I was not there, went on talking to each other,
brushing past me to wash and dry the dishes.
Nothing seemed more terrible, more cruel.
How can I say that, never nagged or beaten
as some are, or thrown out? We have to witness
what was, and those withdrawals, obliterations
planted such deadly fears of being abandoned
that when you made your face go blank and crossed your
legs and never let the jolting coach-tour
bring our bodies into faintest contact
I was cast back into an ancient panic,
sweating in my summer clothes, staring rigid
ahead, though gorgeous trees flashed past the window.
I saw a sole path that led out to ruins.
What did you feel? Ah but I know, exactly.

A MORATORIUM

Let us have no more memories, erase them.
Drive up to the moratorium doors where bouncers
are nailing archivists to hardwood panels.
You will not mention last year's drought, far less the
dinosaurs. 'Only a week ago, I — ' 'Off with his
head.' 'Remember how you used to — ' 'Off with
her head.' 'Once upon a time, children, there were — '
'Off with their heads.' The moratorium period
is one year, and in that year no past tenses
will be allowed. I want to see you all living —
and I mean living — you don't burnish the trumpet
you play the trumpet, you don't knot the quipu
you say this is the eighth of June the day of
sacrifices when we give the past its
obsidian. Runners on the altiplano
are up like jaguars. History's jugular
drips. A calendar snatched by a condor
flutters high and higher till the soaring
days dissolve in hungry sunlight. Gullets
of eternal blue — do you hear me — are terrifyingly,
gigantically, beautifully open.

A FUCHSIA

I rescued it three years ago from rubbish.
Half-dead, a limp ungainly arc of ripped-off
green, it lay without a flower to recommend it
and somehow like a spring or snake it challenged
the logic of the vertical, resisted
potting; but I firmed it, staked it, waited.
Sometimes it's barish, sometimes bushy; tries, though.
This summer it decided to be bushy,
parachutes pushed out, dangling pink and purple,
trembling as container lorries rumbled,
almost nodding to make me say I loved them,
and so I do, you hear that, you strange plant you,
it's true. You don't love me but I sense something —
no I can't be mistaken, it's next to palpable —
you're bent, a down-turned cup-hook, and without propping
you would collapse into the earth you came from,
so why should you keep flowering so gamely —
I can't but think it speaks to me, your living
loaded curve of grace steadily bearing,
but the best bearing, the best blooming, is moral,
or if that cannot be — who am I to say so,
is chlorophyll so dumb — at least I'm sending,
like an antenna — don't shake, I don't mean insects —
waves of encouragement, solidarities of
struggle, gratitude even for imaginary
gratitude, though who knows what a fuchsia
feels, plucked from dump and dust, from a gehenna
to this west kitchen window, rays of evening
and more mysterious light of human glances.

A FLYPAST

Symphonic shreds had just swept off with Schnittke
when two swans flew like spirits past my window.
Russia, music, soul, said the television,
nature, it said, harmony, ideal.
The long necks stretched, smelt their swan lake, laboured
forward till the trees hid them. And eastern,
the television said, Armenian, Azeri
horizontality,·the patterns endless,
keeping western verticals at bay while
voices circle over silent marshes.
Well, I don't know. My startling flyers flapping
so steady and so low over the van-tops,
the hissing wheels, the sirens and the skateboards,
knew where they were going and had shattered
in their rising from some placid water mirror
a harmony too famous, strode the air-streams
to turn how many heads at windows as we
wonder that we ever thought them spirits,
those muscles working, those webs, that eye, that purpose.

A BLACK DOG DAY

Pour, pour down, light like water, any acre,
any square or warren, any crossroads
of this habble will do. Drench them with your searches,
flash-flood the sweating truncheons from their dust-clouds,
fall pitilessly on the tear-gassed babies,
wash us with our lies into the syvers.

TRAM-RIDE, 1939 (F.M.)

How cold it is to stand on the street corner
at nineteen, in the foggy Glasgow winter,
with pinched white face and hands in pockets, straining
to catch that single stocky gallus figure
who might be anyone but was one only;
prowling a few feet — not too far! — glanced at
idly by the patient Cosmo queue, growing
exposed, your watch burning, how long now, yes but,
what, half an hour, some eyes saying, Stood up, eh? —
until the step has to be taken, casually,
you have to stroll off, what's won by staying?
he won't appear (he had simply forgotten,
you didn't know that then), and on the top deck
of a southbound tram you stare into the window
as it reflects a mask about to shake with
ridiculous but uncontrollable tears, a choking
you gulp back instantly, no one has heard it,
shameful — shameful — to be dominated
by such emotions as the busy tramful
of half indifferent, half curious folk would
mock at if they knew, and would they sometime,
in half a century perhaps, accept that love is
what it is, that tears are what they are, that
Jack can shiver in the numbing close-mouth
of missing dates for Jill or Jake, and suffer?

A WATER HORSE

Impossibly a totality of water
dragonlike some force must surely have uttered
creature from underground chaos emerging
shook itself loose of almost clovelike grits and
grouts and with such thrustful bunched mounting
of air as made a bellying of night-clouds
rose glittering and bucketing over mountains
till at last the moon the unconscionable rider
tugged its unbridled hide and slowly cantered
across the universe, a shine upon a
shine, a whinny from a throat of water.

A SUMMER STORM

Sometimes you feel, think you feel, wings like leather
folding and unfolding; you lean on the veranda
facing a roofscape thunder-dark then sunny,
the air electric without rain, the city
pulsing in shifts and shafts of acid violet
and lemon and then that angry grey descending
pregnant with its first weak worm of lightning —
the neighbours have switched on their lights, they're watching
as if they'd never seen a storm break, faces
frowning slightly, two hands on the sill, turning
away or talking over their shoulder. A stringence
broods. You feel if you move you'll be buffeted
by unseen pungent ribbed primeval membranes
that hover from the thunder to the handrail
where they'd be glad to clamp your fists with talons,
you don't know if they're sultry or they're clammy
or are they dusty, scaly, they're black certainly,
they want to wrap and wrap you like a mummy
and make your immobility go deaf to
the thunderburst as it brings all things living,
and brick and concrete too, there's nothing dead here,
to shake and stream in the cleared air of evening.
You lift your face; they've gone; vast freshness rinses.

THE LAST SCORIA

It was well beyond the visible, that furnace.
Nothing lurid played on the assayers.
They sat in white coats at their winking switchboards.
Millions of dead souls crackled in the bonfire
unheard, with unimaginable refinement
breaking down, down, breaking down, breaking
into what delicatest robot tongs would
quietly withdraw from the roaring, something like
loaves as of platinum, set on trays, cooling,
ready to sustain what? whole heavens of
angels, hells of demons? — burn their fingers,
watch it, all the human pain can never
quite be taken out, tongues even of spirits
will sting on the indignant smelt. Controllers
press their final indifferent keys, the raking
begins, of empires, schools of thought, oppressions,
censors, treacheries, secret executions,
stonings, unknown soldiers, vivisections,
the starved, the slag, the sum of that, the scoria.

A CHANGE

I ordered everyone to do some shouting
as we came through the last pass to the city.
Shout what you like, I said, but give it power.
Our worn accoutrements were hanging from us
like rags of the red rain-forest lichen
we'd camouflaged our stealth with when we had to,
but now we were so boisterous, I was, they were,
under high winds that tore the clouds from hiding
and drove us with them through that scrubby valley,
we'd no concealment, needed none, kept calling
backwards and forwards, imitating bird-cries,
shouting at last in unknown tongues, stumbling
unbelted, shorts about our ankles, kicked off
as we raced through the sage and got snakes scattering —
a fang could never take a joke — our laughter
happy to raise not lay the dust, the sage-brush
happy to purple not blanch flashing skin, our weapons
happy to dangle clashing unprimed but priming
our awesome advancing high-yaller charivari.

Towers and real roads, said the field-glasses
I never threw away. It was worth a crescendo
that the roads were so straight, so neat with motors.
I passed the glasses round, they must all see it.
I said we should make it just about midday.
There must be no harmony, no marching.
Each to his own. Some could be quite naked,
others swathed in vine-leaves, monkeys, leeches.
Throats could be roughened by the last bad brandy.
No one needed haranguing. We hurtled into
the outer suburbs in an hour, with cartwheels,
with shouts that I thought totally unmatchable,
with animals, with scent of sage, with kisses
blown to startled children, to forks half-lifted
behind the beautiful windows of their lunchtime.

AT POPPY'S

Karen you know this is *quite* improper.
These eyelashes *were* on my dressing-table.
It's no use telling me you never saw them.
If you're after Monsieur Jack you can forget it,
he likes the natural look. I know you took them,
I'm not accusing you of anything, just
telling you. You're such a slut in waiting.
Fishnets all right, but fishnets with *finesse*, dear.
Hunks have their niceties, they may be shyish —
yes, laugh, it gives you away that, *raucous* —
I said real men are sensitive to details,
and if you *have* to be an understudy
then you must study. Just because you're younger
you won't be jumping rungs, *that* I can tell you.
Get yourself together, get some nous. Darling
don't *sulk*. A quick pout sometimes can work wonders
but I assure you permanent creases downward
from the mouth are *death*, a lower lip thrusting
upward *death plus one*, so re-lax. Now I've
got my eyes back I can sweep you up and
down and well, if you simply stopped cultivating
those passé sultry slouches you'd have something.
Books, that's it, book on head, walkabout.
What's this old thing, a Trollope, that'll suit you —
I can't read titles, never mind, here take it.
Now let me see you walk. The calves! The shoulders!
Tell your body who's the boss. Do it!
Forward. Round. Mind the table! Back. Smiling!
Don't look as if you'd prunes that hadn't worked yet.
Carriage! that's what we want, like in the old days.
Carriage, my dear, as if you'd melt a ballroom
merely by flowing down the stairs in satin,
at the last step twitching a few lightnings
with one hand as you show a shoe, hide it,
and take the floor. Karen you're not listening!

I keep a good house here. What do they pay for —
sleaze queens? You don't want class you're not for Poppy's.
Pick up the book. Once more. Don't *strut*. Walking!

SUNDAY IN EAST MARS

Poems come from East Mars, said Spicer,
and so they do. Our most perjink transmitters,
miniaturized to the last murmur, for protection
against not only probes but all explorers,
push out particles of that strenuous pleasure
you do your best to record. Intermittent
the bursts are, not to be taken for granted.
We want you not to know, and not to manage.
We think you manage far too much. We'd never
send you a scenario, a storyboard, a legend,
but we do and in our own time endlessly will
give you signals that show greater power's
in stories than in story. What is adjustment?
Giving up. What is a whole? A sum of
parts done wrong. Oh if outgrowing of concepts —
we tap our keys with some fervour here — is dolphins
that slice the air into dripping arcs, figureheads
brighter than any boat was ever fixed to,
we think we've seen inexplicable helpers
that might sustain a castaway. Delight is
use and use delight, and when you write you
move the shape of things that millimetre
it needs to breathe, be reassured of living,
not that it ever was not living, but flickers
and shiftings of its great mass are so sanative
it grows, re-forms yet never forms, advances
in its own dimensions.   It is like a Sunday
here. We are very calm. Scarlet nasturtiums
twine with vigorous will between the boulders.
I love to watch them when I'm not transmitting.
We'd send you one, but then you have it, don't you?

AN ATRIUM

At first we loved the plate-glass glare, the car-horns,
the swarthy shoppers and the garrulous market —
I haggled a set of skewers for 'what kebabs would
that be?' you said laughing — but we sauntered
out of the heat at last, through a huge doorway,
into a hall made cool with many fountains,
green with high palms like columns, silver-columned
with steel like stylized palms, a floor of marble,
and faint muzak from unseen grilles drifting
among the water-drops to make real music,
Cage-like, as our shoes clacked in. Above us —
we could hardly not look up — seemed endless —
the vast round space retreated to the plainest
of pure blue domes that only its gentle shining
showed as not the sky we thought we wanted.
We were enclosed in a great peace pretending
to infinity; the infinity of thinking
came to us without pretence, with wonder, gladness,
amazed fall of the shell of self to the marble,
diamond awareness of others like coloured jewels
walking, talking, smoking, smiling slowly
or sitting on stone benches with their papers,
watching their children dip a hand in waters
that had left paradise that very midday
and brought it to them, brought it to them. Surely
we too were moved by gifts we'd never chaffered,
the poor brass toys we clutched had become earnests
of something we would never define, not golden,
not silver, not even green, but only
a murmur, a goodness, a gushing spring, an echo.

WHISTLING

These coal-black horses were not made of water.
Their half-stripped ramrod riders more like androids
than mercenaries bounced in their stirrups, swearing
from mouths like slits, giving invisible nudges
to iron flanks that knew their masters. The horses
clattered across the courtyard for an airing,
heartily slapped by stable-boys, snorting
and farting between snorts, a morning freedom
before kettledrums. Not a beat yet, only skylarks
rising from the long grass all round, and rustlings
half-sensed where the wind picked a grove. The riders
might have eaten larks, but never heard them,
or if they did it entered generally
into a wellbeing they need never examine,
keeping a tight rein with blank mind, but whistling
suddenly, tunelessly through their teeth, almost
interminably at last, hardly more meaningfully
than the field river not far off, rehearsing
what it could not say better, over and over,
yet we might lean to thinking them more human.
Fugitives heard that whistling, froze, and shivered.

A FULL MOON

The moon with its old beauty and blank power,
crisscrossed by unseen unchanging bootprints —
take a curler's broom to sweep your tracks back! —
slinks from left to right above the roof-tops —
I'm watching it, that's my reluctant tribute
to a mass of rock with light on its deserts —
and vanishes steadily beyond a sight-line
that suddenly seems deprived, left in a blankness
greater than the moon's — crane, strain, the house-wall's
got it, someone else's window's filling,
it's all right! — but the mind, magnetized, misses
the dark man gathering sticks in the story,
the rayed craters of reality, the voyage
of an image soldered into imagination
by the megalith builders and those before them,
and if there were giants on the earth, well then,
they would make their bonfires by its brilliance
and shout at it, wading their stormy foreshore.
I rise and switch the light off like a lift-off.

GOLDEN APPLES

Bradbury, we all want to go to the sun, man!
It's in our veins, we want to scoop it cleanly —
everything that seems impossible, we want it —
to tangle with those lavish prominences,
to eat that heat, to get a golden gauntlet,
to lay our heart at the very heart of the matter.
What a bath of neutrinos, would that not cleanse us?
And helium wings to shoot us through the static?
They say it's all gas, but is that really likely?
We have to find some way to fix our footsteps
like plaques of blacker fire in fire. We have to
be there, to have been there, to return if
sometime we should need to. What is freedom —
couch potatoes at the end of the millennium,
a bingo card, a pub harangue, *Neighbours*?
The craft must stand a million degrees, roughly.
Roughly stand, or roughly a million? Both, with
no guarantee! This is not science fiction.
Lateral thinking scrubs refrigeration
as the only hope. Phoenix and salamander
hint heat is conquered by habitatizing,
not fending off. What fish wear macintoshes?
I can see navigators burning like poets,
boiling like Picts without a stitch of armour,
bolts from the blue that run into the unblue,
themselves both it and not it, gold and ungold,
not melted by but melting, staring, into
groves of energy, billets of resurgence.
And where else should they be, our navigators?

FIRES

What is that place, my father and my mother,
you have gone to, I think of, in the ashes
of the air and not the earth, better to go there
than under stones or in any remembrance
but mine and that of others who once loved you,
fewer year on year. It is midsummer
and till my voice broke, *Summer suns are glowing*
I loved to sing and *One fine day* to hear from
some thin wild old gramophone that carried
its passion across the Rutherglen street, invisibly
played again and again — I thought of that person,
him or her, as taking me to a country
far high sunny where I knew to be happy
was only a moment, a puttering flame in the fireplace
but burning all the misery to cinders
if it could, a sift of dross like what we mourn for
as caskets sink with horrifying blandness
into a roar, into smoke, into light, into almost nothing.
The not quite nothing I praise it and I write it.

A PEDLAR

An old man selling joy comes round here sometimes.
His case weighs down, no one seems to want it.
Buttonless coat and battered cardboard stand there
like diffidence made monumental. Promise —
of anything — never seemed further, blanker.
Who would not slam a door on such a scarecrow?
If any lingered, his entire persuasion
was to look at them, hangdog, hand on case-lock,
waiting to be asked to unroll treasures.
Not that way, never that way, hopeless person!
Even his trudging back was not reproachful.
— But anyway there came a day, today, be honest,
when if something changeable bluff bright cloudy
in the air and such a brash sun shouldering branches
recharged his speech I can only imagine —
but he flung open the case and suddenly was saying
'What is not there is hardly worth desiring,
do you not agree? Is it not fine? Others
have said so, whenever I could elicit
a bit of truth from pursed lips. Pursed and zipped is
what I mean! You tell them it's quite costly
they vanish behind their mortises. Pedlars?
No thanks. Yet four wheels to the hypermarket —
get boys to load your boot with wine and salmon —
a shark steak for a laugh, some avocados —
perhaps a large pavlova if *they're* coming —
will not purr back with it, don't be deluded,
since only what you do not want to pay for
is what I have: I do not sell for money.
But if you can lay out a little pain, it's business.
Break a pig of disappointments, frustrations.
An old billfold of hopes deferred? Only
if it aches, aches. Look at what I have here,
this, and these. The price is not beyond you?'
'No no,' I said, 'no, it's not, no, I'll have some.'

A DREAM OF FAIR WATERS

In retrospect, it might have been a throbbing
more than a pounding, but we smelt salt, seaweed,
all those shrimpy crunchy tideline markers,
what could there be beyond the dunes but ocean?
Over the last rise, and down we came upon it,
stumbling through soft sand towards the glitter
of blue and silver that broke over a slither
of stranded kelp-fronds; jumping, calling, whooping
we made it, shoes off, dying for the splashing
that would refrisk us from a week of trekking.
How we swore then, wading light, not water!
It seemed a fearful swick to us so sweaty,
and many said so, though some sat and wondered
how it was done, admiring from all angles
waves that came in only just too even,
with such a finely synthesized deep crashing
it was only just too low to be the sea's. We
had to think it might be radiation,
feet falling off, madness, enemies grinning
beyond the horizon. I said that was nonsense.
— Yes, but you don't have any explanation!
— Why do you think I need one?
                                        On a signal
I led the doubters out into that dazzle.
Our leggings and shirts crackled faintly, painless.
The shore shelved until our heads bobbed blueness —
should we go on? We were dry. It was like living
in a rainbow. It was like living in a catfish.
We were all rather high. As I strained forward
with eyes fixed on a dark shape in the distance
I shouted Back, go back! The light's not holding!
And everyone could see the long black tanker.
Its deadweight churned through what was not not water.

We struggled to the beach and shook our sparks off.
One more lost chance to bag the interfaces!

ANOTHER PLAY

Two by two and one by one they're rising,
leaving the table, maybe pausing in the hallway
to kick a crash out of the gong — a dinner
ended not begun — slamming into a motor
and hurtling half drunk down the icy by-roads
to who knows where. Blasts of dashboard music
thump. They do not know they have been poisoned,
or that each car will smash when the first gripings
begin to screw their guts like waste-disposers.
Their host is in his slippers, piles the dishwasher.
His wife gently sprinkles the wall-length fish-tank
with a few fine-chopped gobbets. Well, what an evening.
When Hamlet and Ophelia were married,
they felt a joint revenge obligatory.
A new Ophelia, spirited, inventive,
devised a supper of reconciliation,
spiced meats, nothing untoward for the taste-buds,
pungent mulled wine to cocker up the snuffles
of a frosty night, and then tooth-tingling sorbets,
liqueurs to make them gasp, the wild palate
cannot tell hot from cold, or for that matter
life from death. Claud, Gertrude, Larry, Polly,
Rose and Gus, ineffably slurringly fuddled,
fumble their lash handstakes, throw back their
thankyous, scarves, hoots, uncomprehended
mouthings that a match could have ignited.
Goodnight, sweet ladies, sweet fellows, goodnight, goodnight.
Ophelia stretches out, her red velvet shaking
with laughter. Hamlet yawns, takes off his apron.
'Let's turn in.' 'Did you switch on the blanket?'
'Of course.' 'I know some who could do with one, though!'
Twelve wheels slide into the land of vengeance.

AN IRAQI STUDENT

Quiet spoken Sabbar Sultan in Basra,
I hope you are well as I am unwarlike.
Belligerent Americans are baking
in Arabia, itching to terrify your cities.
May they not, nor you theirs. But shall we ever
resume new-old conclusions about Titus,
Gormenghast, the great flood, Fuchsia, Steerpike?
The walls are higher now, the roads a minefield.
It would be very bad to be forgetful.
One thin line of thought in words, not shifting
as sands are — well, not quite so shifting, language
shifts with anchors dragging — must manage
like a camel-train to make its measured progress
through missile banks, camouflage fatigues, gas-masks
clustered like decapitated insects —
future ruins already lightly dusted
by the desert wind. I hope you tell your students
of this wet green periphery, of reading
Durrell and Bunting, Murdoch and MacDiarmid,
under Gothic — well, not really Gothic — arches;
add commandeered Strathclyde, as missile-haunted
as now the Gulf is, 'The Bunkers of Glen Fruin'
an unwritten skirl, but anyone can hear it.
Keep safe; the edge is everywhere; all know it.

A MANIFESTO

The futurists took ties to yellow parties.
The futurists thought life a bobby-dazzler.
The futurists made heady love to airships.
The futurists made heavy words go heady.
The futurists got canvas off its hindlegs.
The futurists threw music off its shirtfront.
The futurists gesamtkunstwerked the bolshies.
The futurists shot off montage's visa.
The futurists flew kites up up up endless.
The futurists kept dynamos in kennels.
The futurists had soaring paper cities.
The futurists lie snoring in real cities.
The futurists are dreaming of red pigeons.
The futurists hold hands among the atoms.
The futurists, united, shall never be defeated.
The futurists, united, shall never be defeated.
The futurists, united, shall never be defeated.

A LEAVETAKING

It faded down the valley, out of earshot.
The backs were straight, the music was so jaunty
they must have dwindled braced by sightless wishes.
They wave them off and then they stand there watching,
the wives and daughters, the lovers, the three sisters.
Slowly they turn, when they can expect nothing
to be seen or heard except the dry burning valley
with startling broom-pods bursting to remind them
of life and its undeviating purpose.
They are a part of what it is as daily
and not in crises they are walking, working,
one of them pausing to straighten a small picture
and be left staring into it unseeing
as if it framed another world, a better,
although she knows there's none, and that is better.

A LINTEL

Nobody knows how many times the city
has been rebuilt. People like to live there.
Ten millenniums of impacted boneyards
offer no counter-thrust to the piledrivers
as white-veranda'd skyscrapers, unblasted
yet, rise and flaunt what ancient board-games,
half-understood among the skulls, might bet on,
so well-thumbed is the book of revolutions.
'Would not we shatter it to bits' — or try to,
and find the world is a high-fired clay letter
fused to its hard clay envelope. We break it —
yes yes, of course we do — and lose the message.
The oven roars again, communicating
another time, a later wisdom, templates
of penthouses that will become their own cellars,
home for lobbed grenades and searchlights. We live here!
The sniped-at or the earthquake-dizzy concrete
cracks. No one swears we won't go back there!
Even if it should be bare hands time, the jackals
can roam elsewhere, you have a tent you have a
tower. Time-capsules? Those are for children.
We live and die miles down miles up in faience
and porphyry and oil and steel and denim,
saluting them — what, the ages? — as they melt out,
I don't say what they are, melt out delivering
their more than half misunderstood but fiery
cut of wedges tight across our lintel.

A CROW

The summer grows late, cool, ragged, precious.
Clouds like ungainly brooms are sweeping showers
across the slates. On a dripping lamp-standard
a crow hunches, flaps, hunches. The young painter
with his tin of white sings as he hops in and
out of the rain. The sun bursts what it has been saving
so suddenly, so brilliantly, we are smiling.
It is August still. The leaves hang fast and glisten.
If there were no seasons, who would be singing?
If there was no weather, who would be painting?
If there was no earth turning, we darkly, partly
think, no crow would have a lawn to stamp on,
or Aristarchus any globe to dandle.
As not to be born is worst — a crow will tell you,
a worm will tell you — not to be created
crosses galaxies like a shadow of horror.
But created they are; born, I and the painter;
really wet ruffled shiny black half-happy
the feathers of the raucous-hearted clatterer.

LAMPS

And if anyone should tell our adventures,
remember that the universe has spaces
as well as forms — abysses, deserts, niches,
distances without even time as pedlar
to bring you, if you waited, explanations.
No, we have seen what we have seen, but often
there is a blank you must not fill with monsters.
It is all for what is to come after.
It is for the duguth of firm intent, the voyage
he and she and they must take, and you quiet
but trembling in your chair, rising, following
the light you catch, swinging but never vanishing,
into great deeps, our helmet-lamps, beckoning.

August 1988 — August 1990